LOOK AROUND
TRANSPORT

Clive Pace and Jean Birch

Wayland

How to use this book

Use this book to help you discover things about transport. Try to find out as much as you can. The answers to some of the questions are at the back of the book, but don't look at them until you have tried to work them out for yourself. Some of the questions only you can answer.

Never leave your home or school without first telling an adult where you are going. When you are looking at transport remember to be very careful. Never talk to strangers.

Look Around You

Editor: Marcella Streets
Designer: Ross George

First published in 1989 by
Wayland (Publishers) Ltd
61 Western Road, Hove
East Sussex, BN3 1JD, England

© Copyright 1989 Wayland (Publishers) Ltd

British Library Cataloguing in Publication Data

Pace, Clive L.
Transport. — (Look around you).
   1. Transport services
   I. Title   II. Birch, Jean   III. Series
   380.5

ISBN 1 85210 678 6

Phototypeset by Kalligraphics Ltd, Horley, Surrey
Printed and bound in Belgium by Casterman S.A.

Contents

Answers to questions are on page 28.
All the words that are <u>underlined</u> appear
in the glossary on page 29.

YOUR OWN TRANSPORT

Do you own a bicycle?

Many people like to use a bicycle for transport because it is a cheap way to travel and keeps you fit.

A faster way of travelling on two wheels is by motorbike.

What kind of special clothing do motorcyclists wear? Why do you think they wear these clothes? Do you know why motorcycling can be dangerous?

Only two people at one time can ride a motorbike, but the whole family can travel together by car.

In a car, everyone is protected from the weather. Cars are also safer than motorbikes if there is an accident.

Seat belts help to keep people in a safe position in a car. They stop you from being thrown around if the car crashes.

What kinds of special <u>restraints</u> are there to keep children of different ages safely fastened in a car?

BUSES AND TAXIS

Public transport can be used by anyone who can pay the fare. Buses are a form of public transport. Many towns have minibuses. They are cheaper to run than larger buses and make more frequent trips.

On busy routes where there are a lot of passengers, bus companies use large single-decker buses. In large towns and cities you may see many double-decker buses.

Why are these a good idea?

For long distances, travelling by coach is more comfortable than an ordinary bus.

Some <u>luxury</u> coaches have an attendant who serves drinks and snacks. Sometimes passengers can watch a film during the journey.

Coach passengers often have luggage with them.

Where is it put?

If you travel by taxi, you can tell the the driver exactly where to go. Taxis do not have to keep to special routes or a timetable, as buses do. The taxi fare depends on how far you travel.

It is more expensive to travel by taxi than by bus, but it is more convenient.

How do you know if a taxi is available for <u>hire</u>?

RAIL TRANSPORT

Trains are used for short and long journeys. People who live in the <u>suburbs</u> of a city often catch a train to work in the centre of the city. These people are called commuters. Some commuter trains travel underground.

In other places people travel by local trains above ground. Very often these trains are like a bus service and you pay your fare on the train.

▼

What are the <u>advantages</u> of this?

Inter-City trains are fast and are used for long journeys.
▼

They often have a buffet car.

Do you know what a buffet car is?

How do you think Inter-City trains got their name?

What differences can you see between the Inter-City and local trains?

WATER TRANSPORT

In the past, people used water transport to get across rivers. Now there are very few <u>ferries</u> that take people across rivers.

Do you know why?

This ferry has no engine. ▶

How does it move?

Ferries like this are used to carry people across long distances. ▼

In tourist areas, you might take a trip on a pleasure launch on the river.

Sometimes there is a guide on board who points out places of interest.

AIR TRANSPORT

Aeroplanes are the fastest way to travel long distances.

When you look up and see them in the sky, have you ever thought where they are going?

They fly all over the world. ▶

Some aeroplanes are huge and carry hundreds of passengers between <u>continents</u>.

◀ Pilots of small aeroplanes often fly as a <u>hobby</u>.

Have you been in an aeroplane?

Some people enjoy flying gliders. These have no engines. Air currents keep them up in the air.

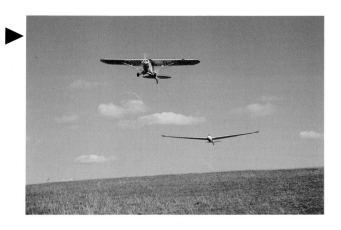

Do you know how gliders take off?

Helicopters are another kind of air transport. They do not have wings. Instead they have <u>rotors</u> which make them fly.

The advantage of helicopters is that they do not need a <u>runway</u> for taking off or landing. They can also fly very slowly or <u>hover</u> above the ground.

When do helicopters hover?

VANS AND LORRIES

Vans are usually used to deliver goods in a small area. They deliver to shops and houses. The sign on the side of the van usually tells you what it is used for.

What do you think this van contains?

Vans make many deliveries to schools.
What vans call at your school?
What are they delivering?

Lorries are used to carry heavy loads over long distances.

Articulated lorries have a cab for the driver, which can be separated from the rest of the lorry. The driver can then connect a different back section to his cab quite easily.

Tankers are specially designed to carry liquids like milk and chemicals.

What else can be carried in tankers?

SPECIAL NEEDS

People who are <u>disabled</u> often need special help to get about. If they find walking difficult, they may have to use wheelchairs. This wheelchair is being pushed by a helper.

▼

Electric wheelchairs have a motor which runs off a battery. The person in the wheelchair can control where it goes.

Why do you think disabled people prefer electric wheelchairs?

Ordinary minibuses and cars can be <u>adapted</u> so that people in wheelchairs can get in.

Minibuses can have a lift put in at the back. People drive their wheelchairs on to the lift. The lift rises and then they drive the wheelchair into the bus.

◀ You might have seen a pavement vehicle like this.

It looks like a small car and travels along the pavement.

Why are pavement vehicles better than wheelchairs?

TRANSPORT IN THE PAST

You can still see some kinds of transport which were used in the past.

◄ Trams used to run on rails through many towns. The power came from wires running above them.

Why do you think buses replaced trams?

Do you know where there are trams still running?

◄ Some firms use horse-drawn drays to deliver their goods.

What are the advantages of delivering in this way? What are the disadvantages?

Sometimes you will see <u>replicas</u> of old vehicles on the roads. These are built specially. They are modern vehicles but are made to look old-fashioned on the outside.

▼

Firms like them because they draw attention to the goods they are selling.

◄ Some people like to travel in a train pulled by an old steam engine. The people who work on a steam railway are not usually paid. They give up their free time because they like working with steam engines.

23

WORK AND TRANSPORT

Many people have jobs working with transport.

Ambulances have two drivers. They are specially trained to give first aid to injured people.

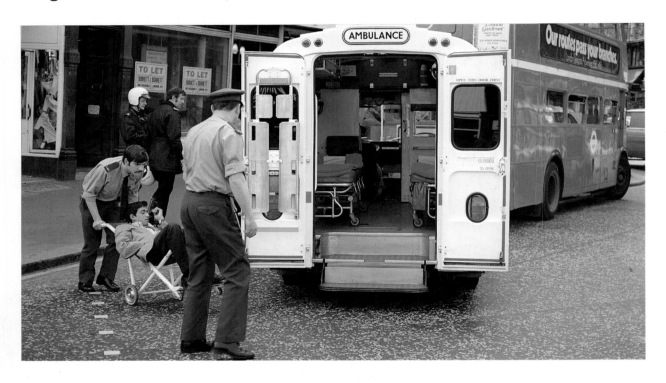

The drivers of breakdown trucks also have special <u>skills</u>. They are <u>mechanics</u> and can repair broken-down vehicles.

If the mechanic cannot repair the car straight away, how is it taken to the garage?

Police cars and motorbikes are often used to <u>escort</u> very long or very wide loads.

The police drive very slowly in front of the lorry and behind it. They keep their lights flashing to warn other drivers that a dangerous load is approaching.

Why are long and wide loads dangerous for other drivers?

UNUSUAL TRANSPORT

In tourist areas there are often unusual forms of transport. You may see buses with open tops. Cities often have these buses for tours. In seaside towns they usually go along the seafront.

Why are buses with open tops a good idea?

◀ Some places have landaus. These are old-fashioned open carriages which are pulled by horses.

Why do people like to travel in them?

Another unusual form of transport is a hot-air balloon.

Travelling high up in the sky, you get a good view of the land below.

Have you ever seen a bicycle like this?
▼

It is pedalled by two people.

Do you know what it is called?

What unusual forms of transport have you seen?

What did you find out?

Page 8:
Motorcyclists wear a crash helmet to protect their heads.
They often wear leather clothes to protect their skin in an accident and to keep them warm.
Motorcycling can be dangerous because the rider has to balance on two wheels and can be knocked off easily.

Page 9:
You may see a carry cot fastened into a car with **straps**, or a **baby carrier** in the front seat. Older children should have their own **safety belt** in the back seat or a special **child seat**.

Page 10:
Double-decker buses can carry twice as many people as single-decker buses, but take up the same space on the road.

Page 11:
Luggage is stored in a special place in the side or back of the coach.
You know a taxi is for **hire** because the 'For Hire' sign is up or the 'Taxi' sign is lit up.

Page 12:
The advantage of paying your **fare** on the train is that you do not have to queue for a ticket, so you save time.

Page 13:
A **buffet car** is the compartment of a train where food and drink can be bought.
Inter-City trains got their name because they travel between cities.
The Inter-City train has a <u>streamlined</u>

shape, so that it can travel faster. It has 'Inter-City' painted on the side and is a different colour from the local train.

Page 14:
There are no longer many river **ferries** because most rivers now have bridges. The ferryman makes the ferry move across the river by winding the cable, which is fastened to the river bank.

Page 17:
Gliders are towed into the air by plane or by a vehicle. **Helicopters** hover when searching for people in danger and when they are lowering or lifting things in awkward places.

Page 18:
This van contains tea.

Page 19:
Petrol, oil and beer are some of the liquids carried in **tankers**. Powders such as flour are also carried in tankers sometimes.

Page 20:
Disabled people prefer **electric wheelchairs** because they like to move about without having to wait for someone to push them. Pushing a wheelchair is hard work.

Page 21:
Pavement vehicles can go further and climb kerbs.

Page 22:
Trams need rails to run on, so you cannot change the route.
Blackpool still has trams.
The **dray** draws attention to the company

and advertises its goods. It can also be cheaper to run than a large lorry in busy streets and there is no air pollution from it. The disadvantages are that a dray is very slow, cannot travel very far and cannot carry as much as a lorry.

Page 24:
The **breakdown truck** can tow the car to the garage using a rope or special frame to lift up the front wheels.
Some breakdown trucks can pull the car completely on to the back of the truck.

Page 25:
Wide or long loads travel very slowly and often take up more than half of the road. They are difficult to overtake safely.

Page 26/27:
Passengers on **open-topped buses** get a better view of the surrounding area. People like **landaus** because they enjoy travelling slowly in an old-fashioned type of transport. The driver can tell them about interesting places as they pass by.
This **bicycle** is called a tandem.

Glossary

Adapted   Changed in a particular way.
Advantages   The good points about something.
Continents   The main areas of the world's land: Antarctica, Europe, Africa, Asia, North and South America, Australia.
Disabled   Being unable to do all the things completely healthy people can do, either because of illness or an accident.
Disadvantages   The bad points about something.
Dray   A horse-drawn cart with a flat platform and no sides which makes it easy to carry heavy loads.
Escort   To go on a journey with someone for protection or as a guide.
Ferries   Boats that carry people over water.
Hire   Payment for using something for a certain amount of time or distance.
Hobby   A favourite interest.
Hover   Stay in the air over the same spot.

Luxury   Something pleasant but not necessary in everyday life.
Mechanics   People who are skilled in working with tools or machines.
Pollution   Dirt.
Replicas   Modern copies.
Restraints   Ways of fastening someone in a car so that they are held safely if there is an accident.
Rotors   The blades on top of a helicopter that turn around very fast and lift it into the air.
Runway   A path used by aeroplanes for taking off and landing.
Trams   Vehicles that run on rails and are driven by electricity.
Skills   Cleverness at something, or training in something.
Streamlined   Shaped to travel easily through the air or water.
Suburbs   The areas where people live at the edge of a city or large town.

Further reading

BMX Bikes by Norman Barrett (Franklin Watts, 1987)
Let's Look at Bikes by Andrew Langley (Wayland, 1989)
Road Travel by Angela Royston (Macdonald, 1986)
The Train by Ray Marshall and John Bradley (Viking, 1986)
Travel by Air by Michael Pollard (Macmillan, 1986)
Water Travel by Bill Gunston (Macdonald, 1986)
Looking at Buses by Cliff Lines (Wayland, 1984)
Looking at Cars by Cliff Lines (Wayland, 1984)

Picture acknowledgements

J Allan Cash 13, 14 (top),15, 16 (left),19 (right), 22 (top), 23 (top and bottom), 27 (top); Barnaby's Picture Library 21 (left), 24 Jean Birch 8 (top); Cephas 22 (bottom); Jenny Matthews/Format 11, Brenda Prince/Format 21 (right); Metropolitan Police 25; C L Pace 9, 10, 12, 18, 26 (bottom); Wayland Picture Library cover,19 (left); Jennie Woodcock 20; ZEFA 8 (bottom), 14 (bottom), 16 (right), 17 (top and bottom), 26 (top), 27 (bottom).

Index